HAL•LEONARD

PIANO PLAY-ALONG

PIANO SOLO • CD

VOLUME 97

T0061373

GREAT CLASSICAL THEMES

ISBN 978-1-4234-9469-0

HAL•LEONARD®
CORPORATION

7777 W. BLUEMOUND RD. P.O. BOX 13819 MILWAUKEE, WI 53213

In Australia Contact:
Hal Leonard Australia Pty. Ltd.
4 Lentara Court
Cheltenham, Victoria, 3192 Australia
Email: ausadmin@halleonard.com.au

Visit Hal Leonard Online at
www.halleonard.com

AVE MARIA

By CHARLES GOUNOD
based on "Prelude in C Major" by Johann Sebastian Bach

Andante con moto

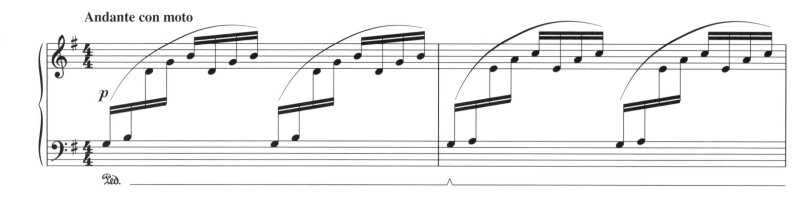

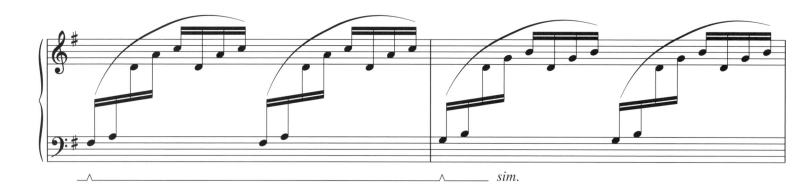

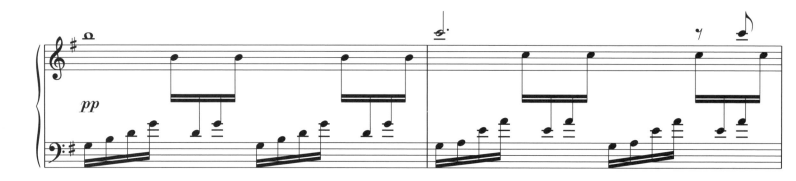

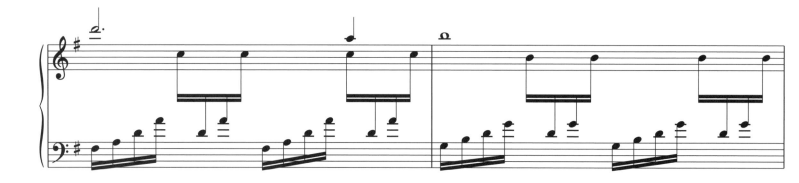

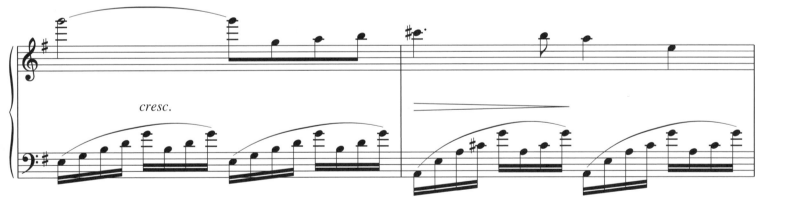

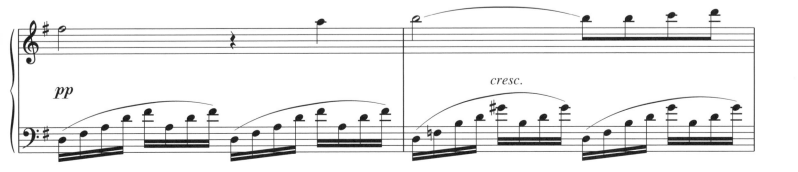

4

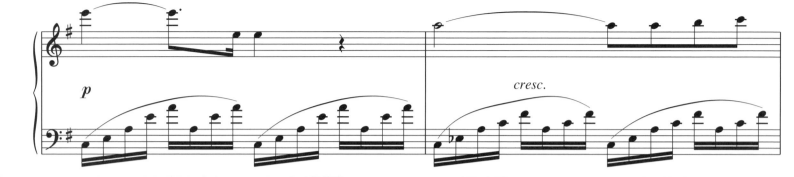

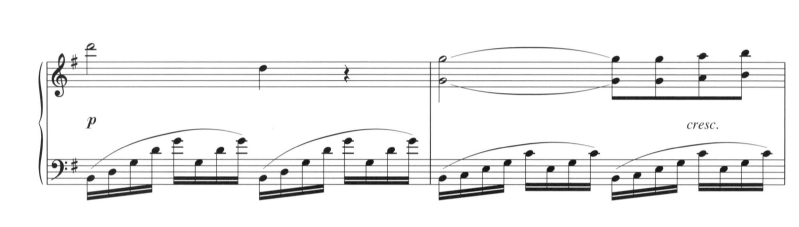

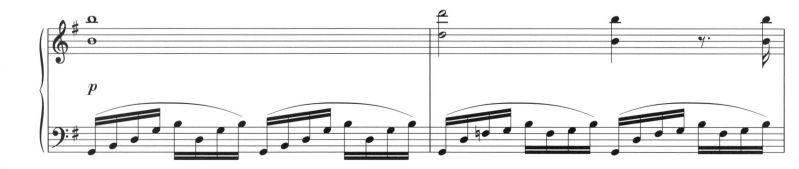

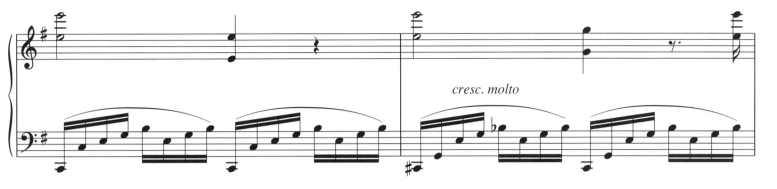

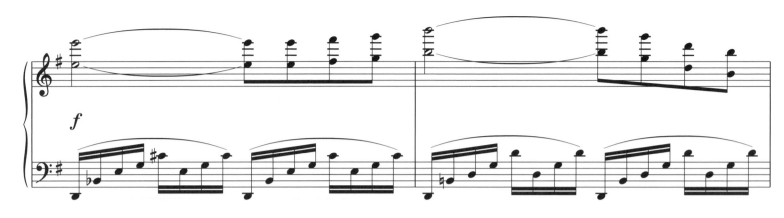

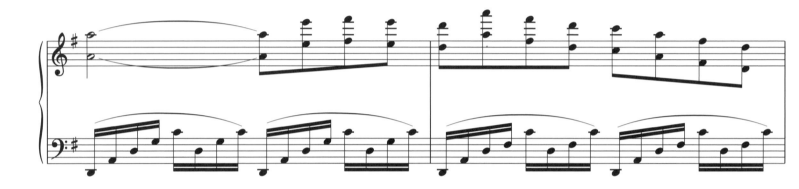

BY THE BEAUTIFUL BLUE DANUBE

Themes

By JOHANN STRAUSS, JR.

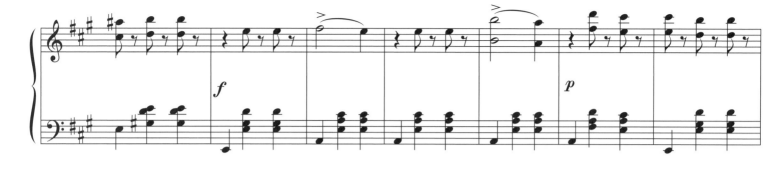

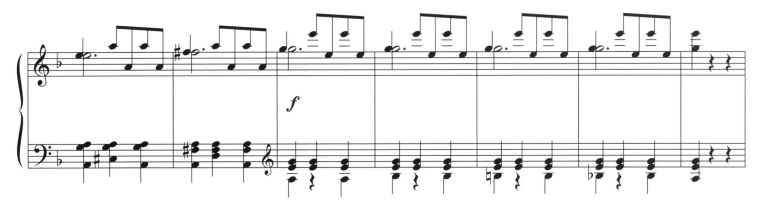

CLAIR DE LUNE

By CLAUDE DEBUSSY

Andante *très expressif (very expressively)*

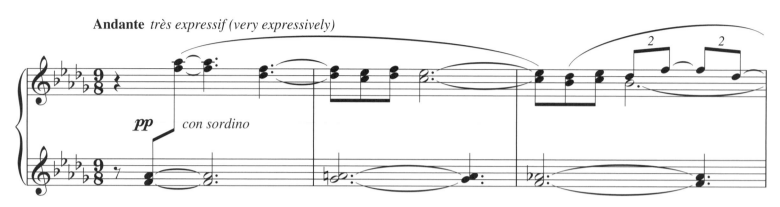

Tempo rubato

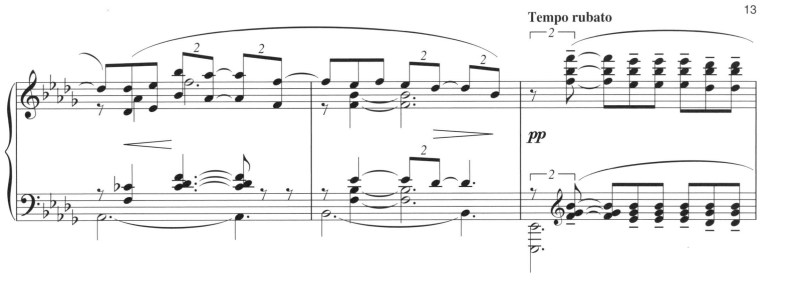

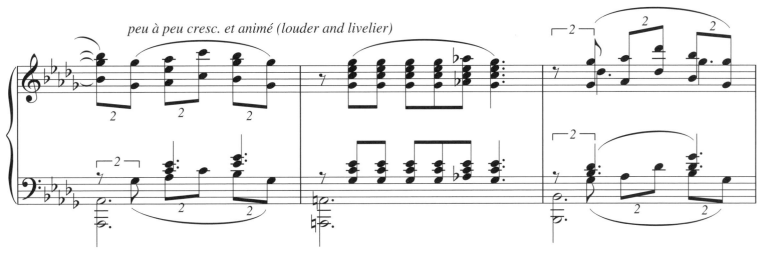

peu à peu cresc. et animé (louder and livelier)

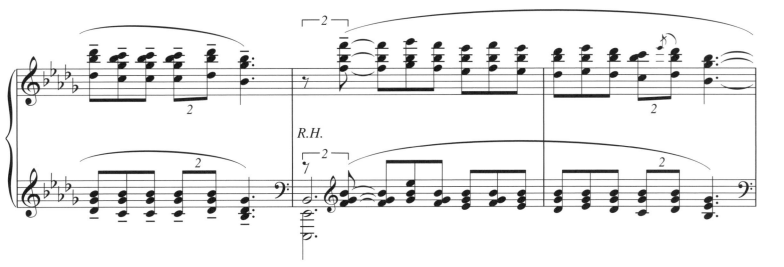

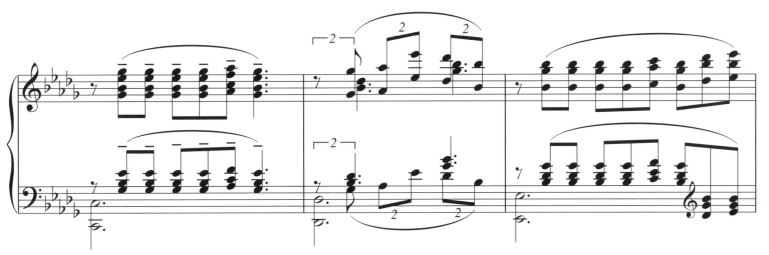

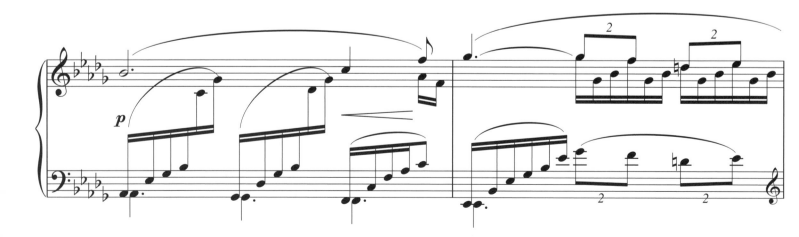

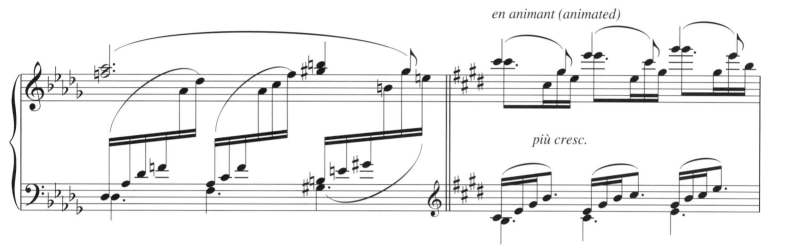

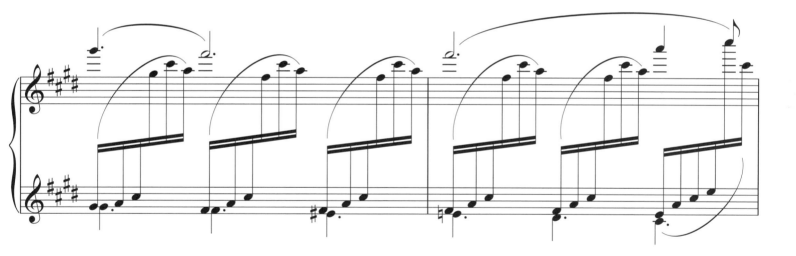

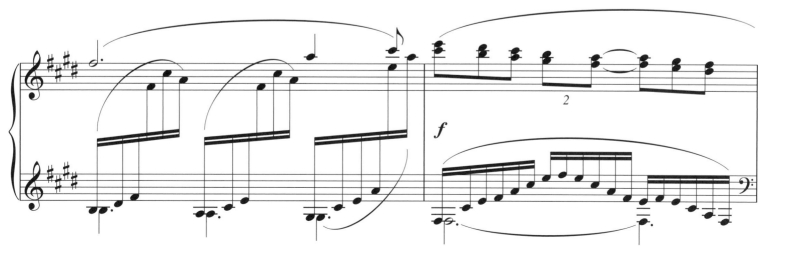

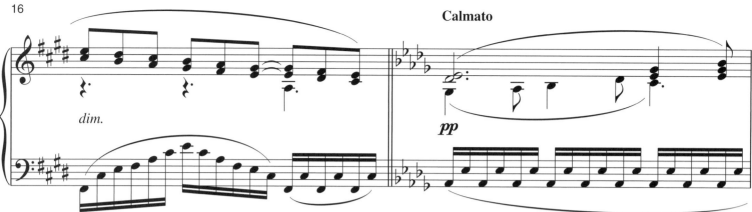

Calmato

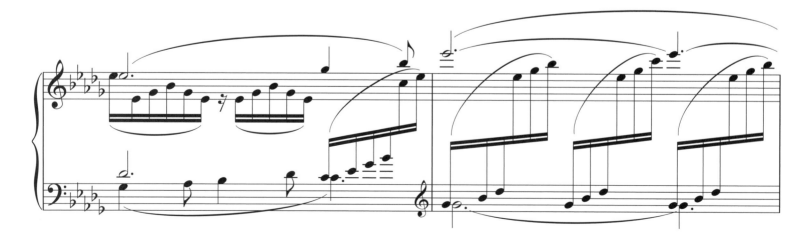

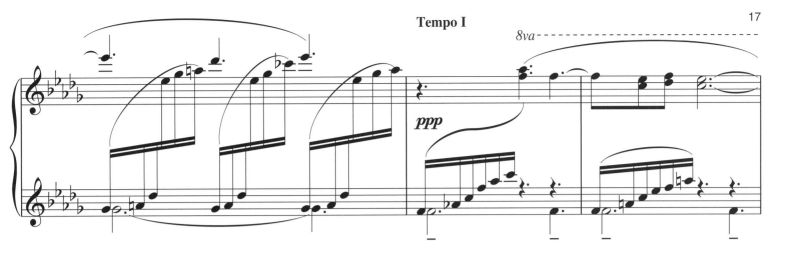

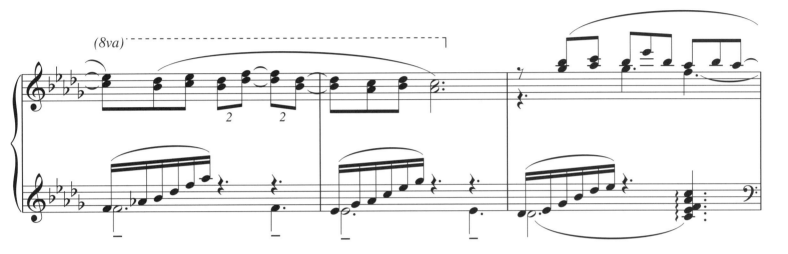

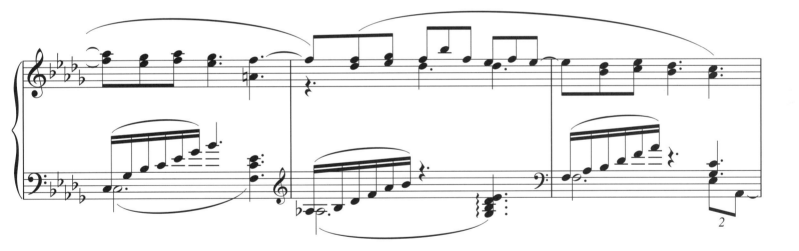

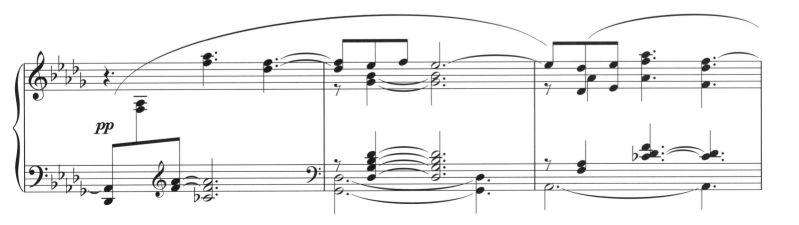

morendo jusqu'à la fin (more and more faint to the end)

EINE KLEINE NACHTMUSIK
("Serenade")
First Movement Excerpt

By WOLFGANG AMADEUS MOZART

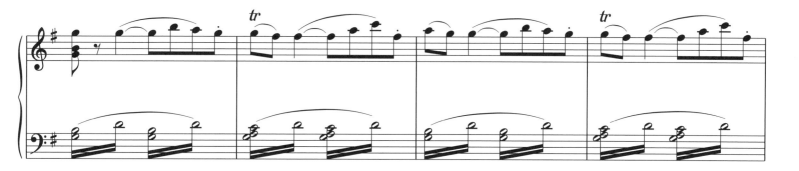

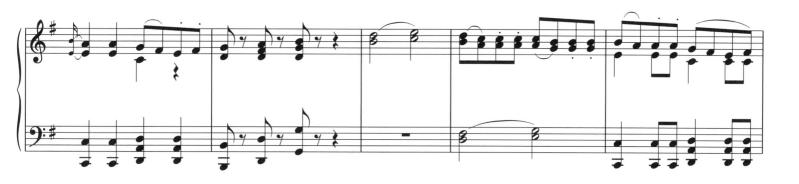

LA DONNA È MOBILE
from the opera RIGOLETTO

By GIUSEPPI VERDI

Allegretto (♪ = 138)

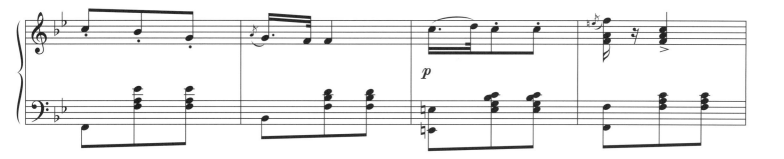

LULLABY
(Cradle Song)

By JOHANNES BRAHMS

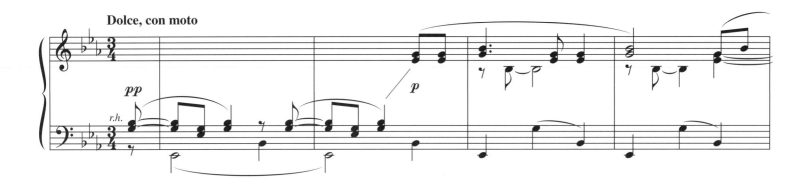

MEDITATION
from THAÏS

By JULES MASSENET

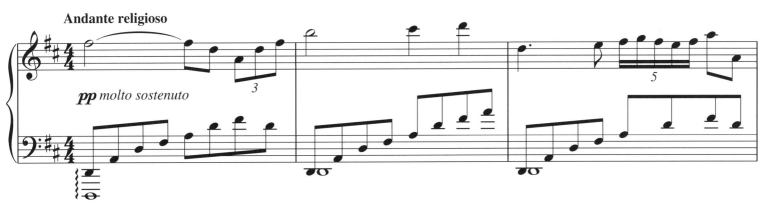

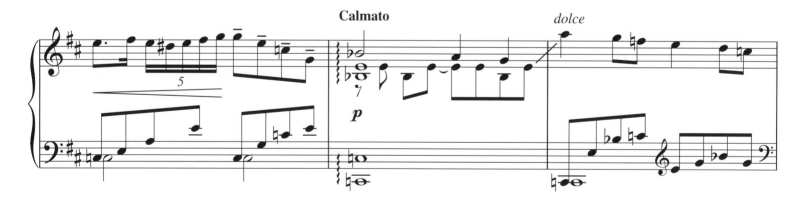

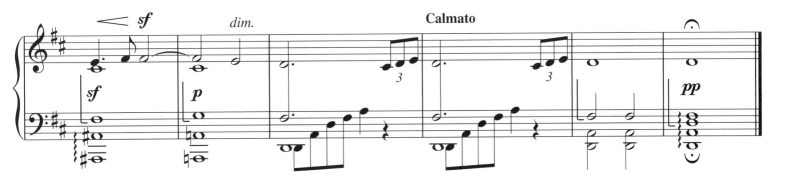

TRÄUMEREI
(Reverie)
from SCENES FROM CHILDHOOD

By ROBERT SCHUMANN

Adagio espressivo (♩ = 56)

With pedal

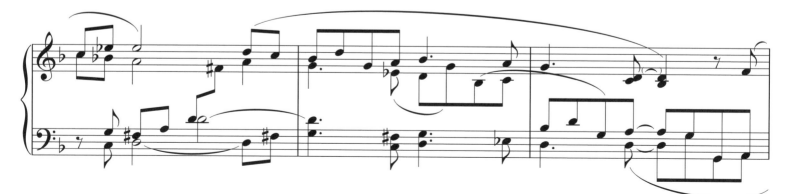

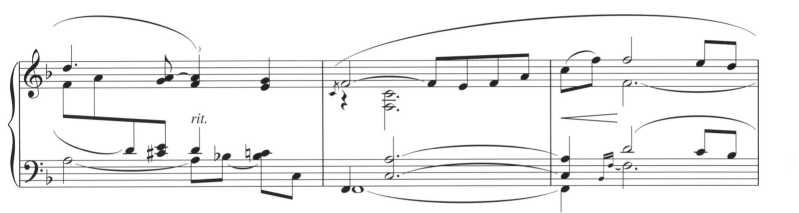

WALTZ OF THE FLOWERS
from the ballet THE NUTCRACKER

By PYOTR IL'YICH TCHAIKOVSKY

Moderate Waltz tempo

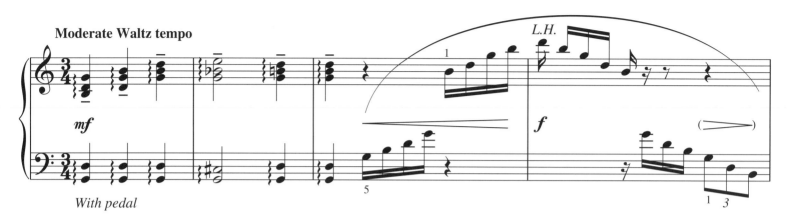

Cadenza, ad lib.

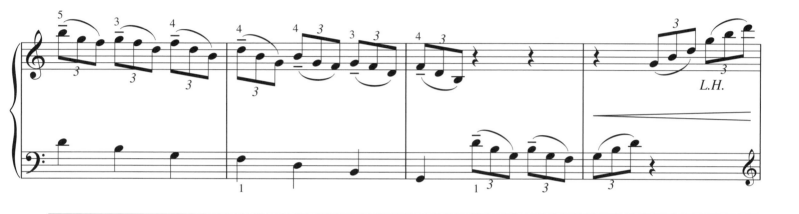

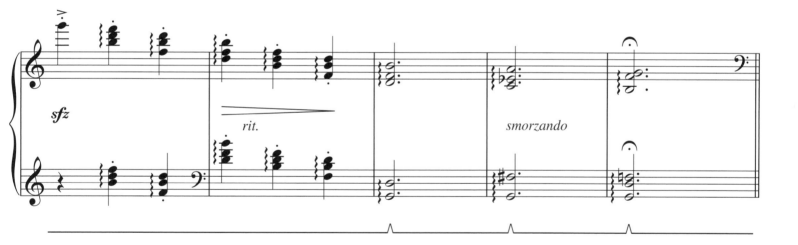

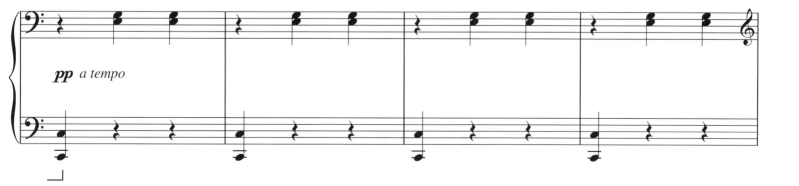

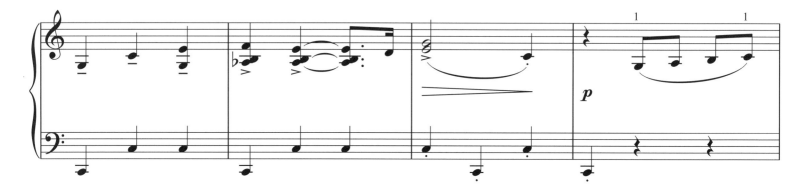

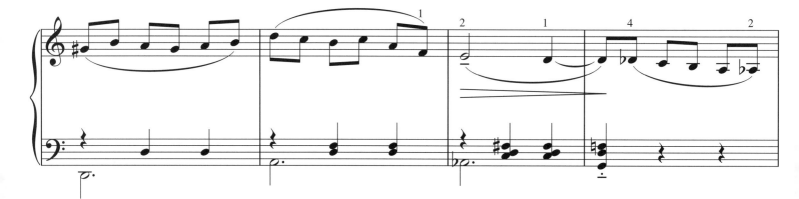

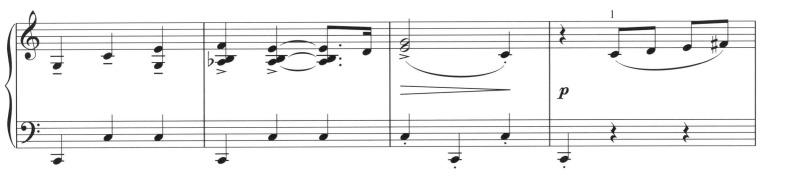

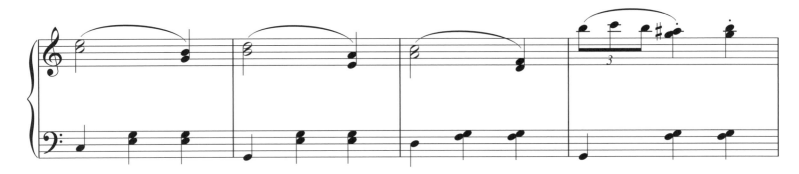

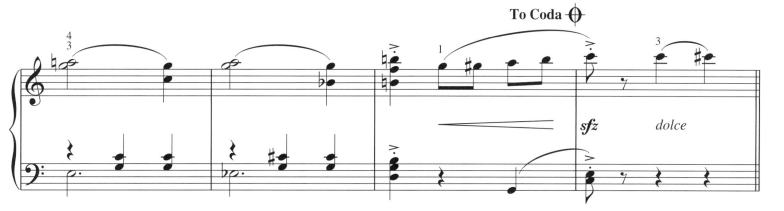

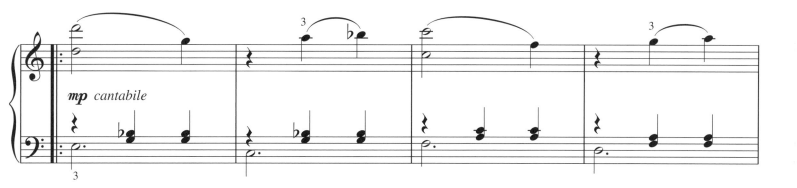

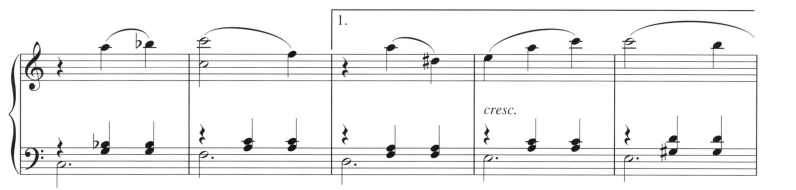

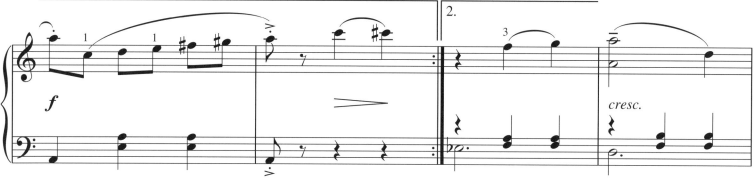

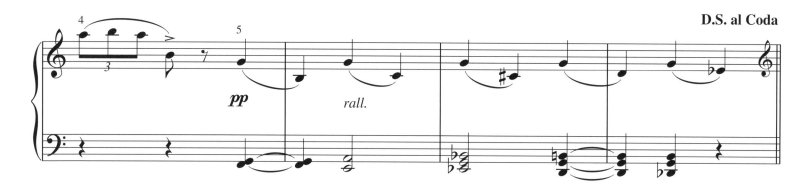

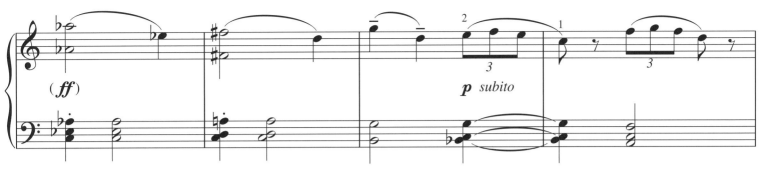

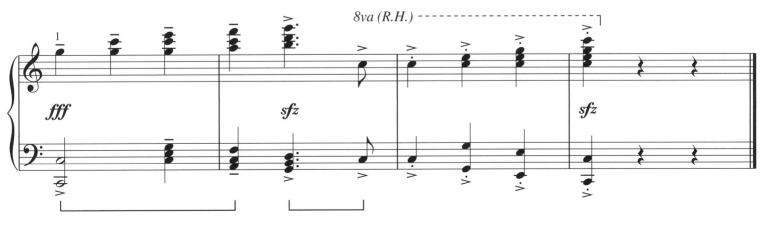

SYMPHONY NO. 9

("From the New World")
Second Movement Excerpt

By ANTONÍN DVOŘÁK

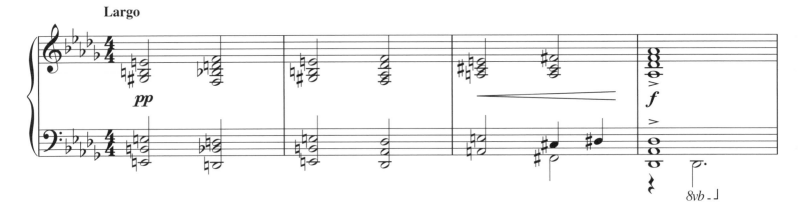

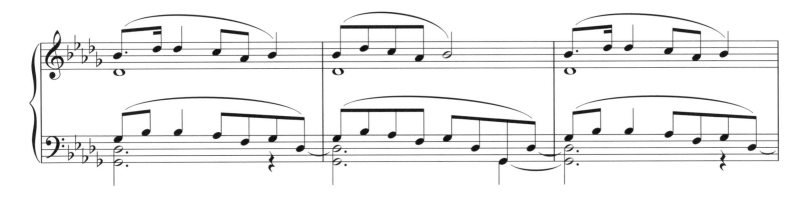

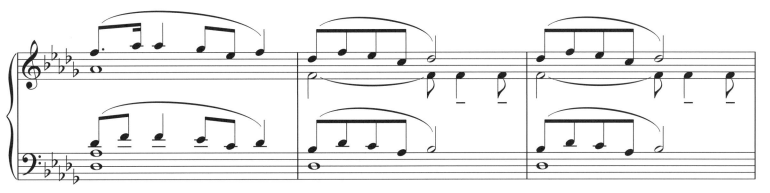

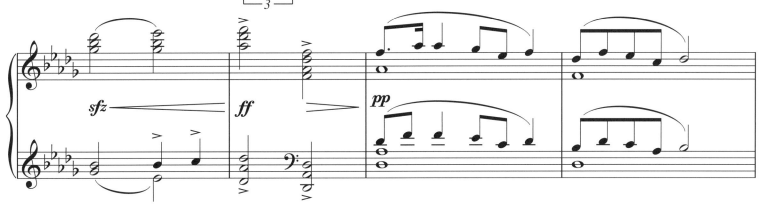

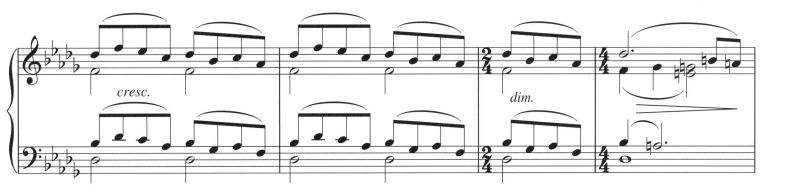

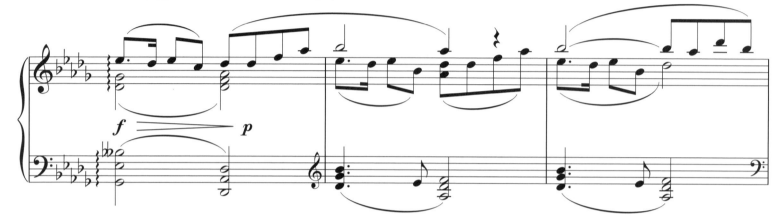

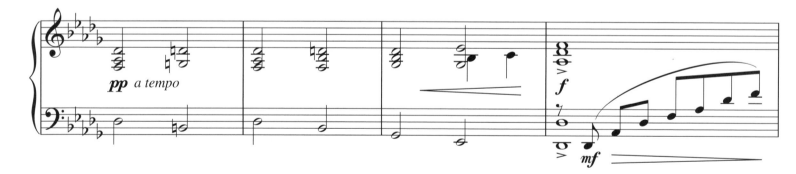

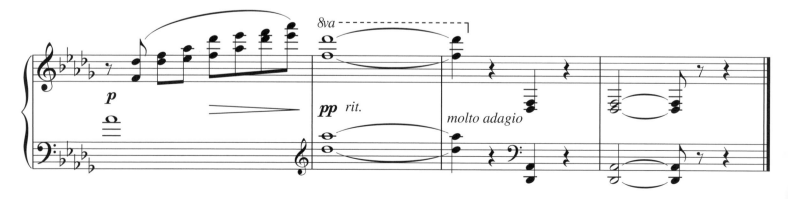